Forex for Beginners

50 Secret Tips and Tricks to go from Zero to Hero in 30 Days

© **Copyright 2016 by Griz Trainor - All rights reserved.**

This document is geared towards providing exact and reliable information in regards to the topic and issue covered. The publication is sold with the idea that the publisher is not required to render accounting, officially permitted, or otherwise, qualified services. If advice is necessary, legal or professional, a practiced individual in the profession should be ordered.

- From a Declaration of Principles which was accepted and approved equally by a Committee of the American Bar Association and a Committee of Publishers and Associations.

In no way is it legal to reproduce, duplicate, or transmit any part of this document in either electronic means or in printed format. Recording of this publication is strictly prohibited and any storage of this document is not allowed unless with written permission from the publisher. All rights reserved.

The information provided herein is stated to be truthful and consistent, in that any liability, in terms of inattention or otherwise, by any usage or abuse of any policies, processes, or directions contained within is the solitary and utter responsibility of the recipient reader. Under no circumstances will any legal responsibility or blame be held against the publisher for any reparation, damages, or monetary loss due to the information herein, either directly or indirectly.

Respective authors own all copyrights not held by the publisher.

Forex for Beginners

The information herein is offered for informational purposes solely, and is universal as so. The presentation of the information is without contract or any type of guarantee assurance.

The trademarks that are used are without any consent, and the publication of the trademark is without permission or backing by the trademark owner. All trademarks and brands within this book are for clarifying purposes only and are the owned by the owners themselves, not affiliated with this document.

Table of Contents

Introduction: Why Foreign Exchange?	1
Chapter 1: The Basics that All Beginners should Know	4
Chapter 2: Tips to Keep in Mind	10
Chapter 3: Tricks to Help you Along the Way	21
Chapter 4: Forex Information you Need to Have	34
Chapter 5: Do This, if you Want to be Successful	42
Chapter 6: Forex Guidelines to Take to Heart	48
Conclusion	54

Introduction: Why Foreign Exchange?

I want to thank you and congratulate you for downloading the book, *"Forex for Beginners: 50 Tips and Tricks to go from Zero to Hero in 30 Days"*.

The Importance of Knowing why you Chose Forex:

You may have already decided the reasons for why you're becoming interested in Forex trading, which elements attract you to it, and what has made you choose to begin trading. In fact, there are probably a lot of reasons, but it's worth noting that the best reason to keep in mind at all times, is financial independence. Everyone dreams of not having to worry about money, about becoming rich, and retiring early. Everyone has their own personal goals for their finances, and it's important to know what yours are. This way, you will stay motivated on the road to success.

The Market Presents Opportunities for Anyone:

The developments of the online world have made the investment market widely available across the world, making it possible for anyone to begin trading online. One main reason for the increasing interest in this subject is the prospect of becoming financially independent, which can be made a reality, with wise and thought-out trading with Forex. Whether you are a teacher, journalist, doctor, or business executive, you can start getting involved with and benefiting from this market.

You can choose to either supplement your income with what you earn from playing in the Forex market, or you can even dedicate all of your time to it and make it your main source of income. When you are first starting out, it's recommended that you only do this as a side gig until you master your skills. Many people end up having a successful career dedicating their time to this pursuit, so it's perfectly possible!

The Benefits of Being your own Boss:

When it comes to making money with the market, you don't have to answer to a manager or follow orders all day. You answer to your own decisions and are free to do as you wish. If you need a vacation, there's no one to ask for permission, and you could even work less hours and retire early. Does this sound good to you? Then read on to find out about the fundamental aspects beginners need to know about for success in the Forex market. What follows are 50 tips and tricks to allow you to profit from the market. In the first chapter, we will cover some basic, starter information about the market, and then get down to the tips in the following chapters.

In addition to the 50 tips and tricks, you will receive useful general guidelines, along with the basic definitions, terms, and concepts you should be aware of before starting to trade. This guide is a valuable first step in your journey to financial freedom and success. When it comes to the foreign exchange market, there is no limit to how high you can go and how much you can achieve, so let's get to it.

Thanks again for downloading this book, I hope you enjoy it!

Chapter 1: The Basics that All Beginners should Know

For the average citizen who is not yet involved in the Forex market, it is quite simple to explain what Forex means with the example of visiting foreign countries. When a visitor arrives in one country, you need money to buy necessities. This means that you must first get some foreign currency, by exchanging the currency of your home country. Even this simple act technically means you are participating in the market of Forex (the exchange of one currency for another, or "Foreign Exchange"). This term can also be called the international currency market. This type of exchange is not like others.

What Sets Forex Apart and Makes it Unique:

- **It Exists Everywhere:** Geography and time zones have no effect on Forex. While other markets may have open and closing times, this does not apply here. Although it is closed on the weekends, the differing time zones that the market exists across means that it is always open somewhere in the world.

- **The Market Stays out of Monopoly Control:** While other trading markets can fall prey to monopoly control, this cannot happen with Forex.

Even though countless various participants invest in this market, none of them end up dominating or controlling it.

This may lead you to wonder what exactly gets exchanged using Forex. Actually, the answer is "nothing", even though it may seem unbelievable at first glance. Any instrument involved here, even the currencies which are most popular, are not exchanged physically on the Forex market. People who participate simply engage in bets with each other on the changes that will occur in the currency, allowing for a safe margin many times less than what actual volumes are involved in this betting. Later on, one person will pay another person the amount that was gained (a method which is called margin trading).

The Rates of Currency Constantly Shift:

Currency rates are changing and fluctuating constantly, which is the result of many different reasons and factors. Because of these fluctuations, it is possible to profit and earn from trades which are only speculative in nature. Foreign Exchange is the most active and largest market in the world. Every day, the market is in session, not including weekend days. The trading volume involved in Forex hits at least $5 trillion each day.

Which Groups make up the Forex Market?

Overall, the market of foreign exchange is made up of four separate groups.

- **The Central Banks:** The United States Federal Reserve, the Bank of England, and the Central Bank.

- **The Major Banks:** For example, JP Morgan, Barclays Capital, Citigroup, and HSBC. These are the participants in the market that are the most influential.

The entire community of banks which deals with credit operations and the currency exchange makes up a market called inter-bank. The point of these players in the market acting as central banks, is to adjust the rates of currency, not to get a profit. This results in the adjustment of countries' economies. Many times, deals are made by central banks using, major commercial financial institutions, which conceals their actions. This makes it quite obvious that the banks belonging to this particular group do not just make deals, but control prices of their own currency.

Who are the Market Makers of the Forex Market?

People who actively participate in this market work with millions of US dollars and are making trades using their own currency, rather than money that has been borrowed. The participants in Forex who make deals and offer specific prices of nearly infinite volume are known as the market makers.

Participants for Investing and Deals for Business:

Another layer of this market is reserved for insurance, investment, funds for pension, large corporations, and banks of a medium size. These participants in the market undergo operations for currency exchange, in order to fulfill investment goals and make deals for business. They also do this for the purpose of speculations in the long term. "Quantum" by George Soros is one of the world's largest funds for investment. Funds are known to attract huge amounts of money in borrowings and are able to withstand central banks' intervention on the market.

The Financial Companies involved in Forex:

Another group involved in the foreign exchange market is the companies of finance. Actually, they act, between the market and individuals, as intermediaries. This refers to individuals that are both legal and physical, and the form another group in the foreign exchange market. Actually, companies have finance have managed to overcome barriers to engaging with the market, for individual investors. Not only this, not the development of the internet has made services for brokerage widely available for people across the globe.

Why do Investors Choose Forex over Other Investment Avenues?

- **Market Liquidity:** It's a highly liquid market: The market of foreign exchange differs from the ones where participants purchase and sell items or property. For example, take the scenario of trying to sell of your apartment. When searching for just a second or two, you cannot find any buyers at all. When you dedicate an entire day to the pursuit, you may be able to find five tops.

    The foreign exchange market, on the other hand, is not stuck with these limits. Traders can make deals and open whatever positions they want in a matter of seconds. Liquidity in Forex is an appealing factor for investors, since you are able to trade using the volume you choose.

- **Accessibility:** Since the market is constantly operating somewhere in the world, you can access it any time you wish, as opposed to the market of stocks, which limits you to open hours of trading. Trading on the stock market may be out of sync with the time zone you live in, making it highly inconvenient to pursue this avenue. Traders of foreign exchange, however, need not wait around to make moves on unforeseen occurrences, the way players in other markets must. You can choose when to trade; during the nights, after your day job, or in your free time.

In order to trade, you only have to have a mobile or a computer, and connection to the internet. Remember that the market is closed on the weekends, which means you should try to wrap up your deals by Friday evenings.

Chapter 2: Tips to Keep in Mind

Now that we've covered some basics about the market of foreign exchange, we can get down to the 50 tips and tricks. Using these guidelines, you will be well on your way to success and financial independence.

Tip Number One: Know the Opening and Closing Hours of the Market Sessions.

In order to become successful with Forex, you need to know what hours you can use it. The market of foreign exchange operates five days a week, as mentioned earlier. But there are three separate market sessions to be aware of. These are the American, European, and Asian sessions. The times are as follows:

- **The American Exchange Market Session:** This session opens in New York at 8 in the morning Eastern Daylight time, and closes at 5 pm Eastern Daylight time.

- **The European Exchange Market Session:** This is located in London, England, and opens at 3 am Eastern Daylight time, closing down at noon.

- **The Asian Exchange Market Session:** This is located in the capital city of Tokyo and opens at 7 pm Eastern Daylight time and goes until 4 am Eastern Daylight time.

Out of these three, the most active of the sessions is the European session. The least active session is the one in Tokyo, and the American session lies somewhere in the middle. Participants in the market must trade when there are high activity times on the market, when the major exchanges across the planet are trading. This increases access to helpful macro-economic data, which contributes to successful trading of foreign exchange. You can find this information online, at financial companies' websites, using the economic calendars listed there.

Tip Number Two: Utilize Brokerage Firms for Forex Trading.

You might now be wondering how, exactly, you should go about getting familiar with the market of foreign exchange. Brokerage firms are valuable resources, especially to beginner traders. Even if you hope to be an independent trader at one point, starting out here can be helpful for you. Brokers allow small time investors access to opportunities to begin operations in the foreign exchange market. Here is the basic process of finding a broker to become a client of:

- **Start an Account with a Deposit:** To start an account, you must begin with some capital, known as a deposit. The requirements for these deposits are different depending on the broker you use. For example, some markets ask for just one dollar to begin trading.

- **Leverage with the Company:** In order to attempt to increase the profits of their clients, all companies sets up a certain level of credit, also known, in the trading world, as leverage. The amount that was deposited gets multiplied by the size of the leverage, allowing traders to trade using a higher amount. If the investment loses, they will only lose the money that they put forth themselves (the one dollar, for example).

Tip Number Three: Get Acquainted with Cost Definitions.

In order to trade successfully, you have to know a fair amount of terms, so we will start with the basics. These are the ask price, the bid price, and the spread.

- **The Ask Price:** This is the price that an investor (or client, when using a broker) makes purchases with.

- **The Bid Price:** This refers to the currency that a client makes sales with while trading.

- **The Spread:** The spread refers to whatever difference remains between the ask price and the bid price. This can differ a lot depending on the state of the pair of currencies. Typically, an investor will prefer a low spread to a high spread, since it has an effect on how the trade will go.

    Spreads are higher amounts for currencies which don't get traded as often, meaning that spreads between the most popular, major currencies tends to be lower. Brokerages offer fixed and low spreads to their customers.

Tip Number Four: Know what your Goals are.

To accomplish any goals, you first have to know what those goals are. Take some time to define what your personal financial goals are, and make sure that your lifestyle and personality match with the trading style you go for. Before someone begins a journey of any kind, they should have an idea of where they want to go and the method for getting there. In order to stay motivated with investing and trading, you need to have your goals specifically defined.

Once you have your objectives clearly stated (for example, save for a vacation, start a college fund for your kids, or retire at 40 years old), you can make sure that the method you choose for trading aligns with these goals. If your personality does not match the trading style you choose, it will only lead to losses and disappointment. For this reason, you should tackle this concern early on in your investing journey.

Tip Number Five: Understand the Concept of Currency Pairs.

This is an important one. Currency pairs are at the base of what it means to trade foreign exchange. All currencies in the foreign exchange market are quoted (priced) and traded using currency pairs (for example, the Great Britain pound or GBP, and the United States dollar or USD). This is due to the fact that in trading, investors have to sell off a currency to purchase another one. The opposite is also true. The first currency listed in a pair, such as GBP/USD is called the base currency, and the second currency listed in a pair is called a quote currency.

- **Opening a Buy Position:** Once a trader buys a pair of currencies (purchased a specific volume of the base currency and purchased it using the currency that was quoted), this is called starting a buy position.

- **Closing a Buy Position:** When a trader sells that same pair of currencies back in the future (or will sell off a similar amount of the base currency, getting the currency that was quoted in exchange), this is known as closing a buy position.

- **Opening a Sell Position:** Similar to this, when traders sell off a pair of currencies (meaning that they have sold a specific amount of the base currency, purchasing it using a quoted currency), this is known as opening the sell position.

- **Closing a Sell Position:** When the trader has purchased that same pair of currencies (meaning that they bought a base currency in the same amount and did this using the currency that was quoted), it's known as closing the sell position.

It is important to note that traders don't need to worry as to where they will take base currencies in order to open sell positions. They also need not worry about opening a currency that has been quoted for a position of buying.

Currencies used here are temporarily given by a company that the trader has opened an account with. When the trader opens a position of buying, they will conduct their trades and related decisions using the currency price (or rate of exchange), which gives the information needed about the amount of unites required to purchase a nute of the base currency, using the units needed of quote currency.

When it comes to positions of selling, also, the choices are made in accordance with the rate of exchange, which will review the amount of units the trader will need of a quote currency. They will then receive these when selling off a single unit of the currency that is the base. When you purchase a currency pair, it should be at the time that you think it will grow in value so you can sell it when it starts to go down in value.

Tip Number Six: Learn to Appreciate your Small Losses in Trading.

You should focus solely on the action of trading and figure out how to appreciate it when you experience losses (small losses, that is). As soon as you have adequately supplied your account with funds, the next important factor to keep in mind is that your capital is always at risk, to a degree. This means that your money shouldn't be necessary to pay your bills or to cover general living costs.

Each time you suffer a small loss, you learn something. This is an especially important attitude to adopt early on in your trading education and journey. What makes or breaks successful traders, and separates the winners from those who give up too early, is that they see losses are chances to get better. Every time you make a mistake, make a note and be grateful that you know what to watch out for.

Tip Number Seven: Start Seeing the Money you Trade with as a Vacation Fund.

Think about the money you trade with as money you would use toward taking a vacation. As soon as you come home from your vacation, the capital has already been spent and is gone. This is the same mental outlook you should apply to your trading pursuits, especially in the practice and beginner stages.

- **A Prepared Attitude:** Adopting this attitude will prepare you psychologically for the inevitable losses you will suffer in the beginning. Accepting these small losses is essential to learning effective risk management techniques.

- **Focus on Acceptance:** Don't count your equity constantly, but instead accept your losses and you will enjoy a lot more success with your trading in the future. Keeping a cool head is non-optional for being successful in trading. Later on in this book, we will discuss the importance of your attitude with trading on the foreign exchange market.

Tip Number Eight: Study Currency Lists to Learn What you're Dealing with.

Forex for Beginners

In order to win on the foreign exchange market, you have to know exactly what you're handling each time you make a trade. This includes knowing all of the abbreviations for the currencies, as well as exactly what they stand for. The main point of Forex trading is using currency. These currencies are displayed using ISO codes, or Latin symbols, which is a global practice now. The codes consist of just three characters, with the first two representing the name of the country, and the last representing the name of the currency.

There are some major currencies that are traded more actively than others on the Forex market. They are:

- **The EUR:** This is the abbreviation for the Euro, or the international currency of Europe.

- **The USD:** This stands for the United States dollar and refers to the currency used in America.

- **The CAD:** This is the dollar used in Canada.

- **The AUD:** This is the dollar used in Australia.

- **The GBP:** Great Britain's currency is called the Great British Pound.

- **The JPY YEN:** The currency of Japan is called the Japanese Yen.

- **The CHF SWF:** Another strong, major currency is the currency of Switzerland; the Swiss Frank.

Other forms of currency used in the market are called "Minor Currencies". Also, the currencies known as Commodity come from those nations, which use export for internal trading, using metals, gas, and materials or oils. There is, in fact, a huge range of these types of currencies, but for a beginner, you should first focus on the New Zealand dollar, the Canadian dollar, and the Australian dollar.

- **Major Currency Pairs:** Also, there's a specific classification of pairs of currencies when they are involved with the USD. Pairs of currencies that are considered major are the pairs that have the USD as either the quoted or the base currency. These pairs are more appropriate for beginner traders.

- **Cross Currency Pairs:** When a pair of currencies does not have the USD in either the quote or the base currency, they are referred to as cross pairs. These pairs are more appropriate for traders who are quite experienced, since extensive economic knowledge is needed to do this effectively. GBP and EUR, or EUR and JPY are both examples of cross currency pairs.

Tip Number Nine: Create Feedback Cycles of Positivity.

As a beginner trader, you should focus on creating positive loops of feedback with your trading pursuits. These can be created from executing trades well by using your pre-planned actions. When a trader carefully maps out their actions, and then follows through with them, this makes a positive pattern of feedback for the trader.

The idea here is that success feeds on success, and that turns into more confidence, particularly when you experience a profitable trade. It shows that all of your hard work, study, and persistence is paying off. Sure, you may have to accept small losses here and there, but if you do this while following your trade plans, you can still create this loop of positivity.

Tip Number Ten: Know, and Take of, Advantage of Leverage.

Every trader has a chance to conduct their trades using higher volume, because of the leverage they will get from their broker. Leverage is the chance to earn profits from big market positions, with relatively low costs (margin). The size of leverage will depend on which company you go with, since differing companies use differing sizes. Some limitations on leverage exist, dependent on the type of account and the deal size and volume.

More Information you should Have: Technical Analysis.

Every successful trader should be aware of technical analysis. This refers to an analysis method that is based on the belief that exchange rate trends can be seen in the fluctuations of those rates from the past. The basis to this belief is that history repeats itself and that complex objects (like the market) are predictable. Traders who use this method of analysis build currency rate charts, figure out the liens of trends on the charts, figure out shapes of reversals of trends. They then calculate different indicators, using the information gathered to choose whether they should open short or long positions (buy or sell).

- **100 Percent Accuracy is Never Possible:** Beginner traders need to understand that predicting these trends in a concrete way is not possible, since the influences on these conditions are complex, political, psychological, and more. Unfortunately, there's no objective law that determines how the market will move, that we can use to make predictions that are always correct.

    However, you can get familiar enough with this process to where you can use technical analysis to benefit your trades. As always, when you're starting out, you should test out your predictions using "paper money" (by writing down what choices you would make for a trade, without investing actual capital). Then you can see whether your predictions were correct, which will allow you to improve and know what to avoid next time.

Chapter 3: Tricks to Help you Along the Way

When it comes to investing in Forex, studying your terms and deciding upon your habits is important. However, no matter how much you know on this subject, being prepared is the only way to excel. Here are some ways to help ensure that you are, so that you can enjoy great success in your trading pursuits.

Tip Number Eleven: Do Analysis on the Weekends, too.

You should always plan ahead for your weekly investments. This means that even when the Forex market is closed (weekend days), you should be studying charts to find news or patterns that could have an impact on your trading. Maybe the news and pundits are saying that the market will be reversing soon, just as a pattern is showing trends that appear to support this theory. Or perhaps the news and pundits are notifying people that the market is near explosion. This could mean that they are attempting to get you to invest so they can more easily sell given the heightened liquidity. These considerations are important to recognize so you can accurately try to form your plans for the week of trading coming up.

- **Only Enter when Conditions are Right:** When you're able to keep a cool head and an objective attitude, your plans will be most successful. Wait until you are seeing the qualities you decided to look for before entering the market. If it turns out the market hasn't reached this point, practice restraint and wait it out.

- **Don't get Disheartened if you must Wait Longer:** You may find that you must wait longer than you thought or hoped for. If you do end up missing a golden trading opportunity, keep in mind that more opportunities will always appear. If you stay disciplined and patient, you will make an excellent trader.

Tip Number Twelve: Know the Numbers and Equations.

Essentially, pairs of currencies get traded in unit volumes of 100,000. These units are standard lots (base currency, in other words). They can also be either mini lots (10,000 units) or even as low as just 1,000.

- **A Standard Lot:** This is 100,000 units.

- **A Mini Lot:** 10,000 units.

- **A Micro Lot:** 1,000 units.

Long Positions: Whenever a new position is opened, a trader must figure out whether they want to start a position of sell or buy. If the trader decides to purchase a base currency while selling a currency that has been quoted, that means that they are hoping that base currency will go up in value, so that they can sell it again for more money.

Short Positions: However, if your wish is to sell off a base currency in hopes of purchasing the quote currency, that means you are hoping the base currency will go down in value so you can buy it for cheaper.

An easy way to remember this information is to keep in mind that selling = short, while buying = long. When it comes to currency prices, they are typically referred to as rates. You should also know that in foreign exchange, each quotation comes with two different prices, the ask and the bid prices. These pair prices are typically displayed with a "/" symbol in between them, with the buy rate listed first.

Tip Number Thirteen: Develop a Patient Attitude.

As soon as you get familiar with what you can come to expect from the methods you use, you need to develop patience for conditions to match your decided-upon entry points and exit points. If you have taken the time to decide to enter markets at a specific level, but find that the market never gets there, it's time to move on and find another opportunity. Don't lower your standards according to momentary concerns. Other trades will always come up and you will find one that matches your specifications.

Tip Number Fourteen: Be Prepared for Tax Season.

Something that a lot of new traders in Forex forget is reporting their taxes. Since it's a global industry with unregulated conditions of the market, the dealers involved don't give out any tax documentation to the country where the trader resides. Reporting taxes is the obligation and responsibility of the one doing the trading. Here is some more useful information to know about the topic:

- **Transaction History:** Dealers will give histories of transactions listed in a detailed, electronic way. This is the information from which investors need to craft their own reports for tax purposes.

- **Find a Dealer with Quality Reporting:** Since this is the norm, selecting a platform for trading that is flexible and organized in their reporting is ideal. However, the quality of this can differ a lot between dealers. While all of Forex dealers will give you full reports of transactions, the way they are listed could be as simple as handing it over to your tax accountant, or to spending hours of your time trying to decipher it.

    Many traders do hundreds of trades annually, so having a platform that can translate that information into an income statement that is easy to understand, at the end of the year, is crucial. Although reporting is not the most fun part about trading Forex, it must be done for your records, and having that information handy can pay off in the long run, come tax season.

- **What to Expect at Tax Season:** The way you will go about your taxes, when it comes to trading currency, depends a lot on your tax status as an individual. It is not the place of dealers to give you tax advice, since it is not their area of expertise. Before going through with any particular action, you should get a hold of a professional for tax purposes. As you get familiar with different platforms of different dealers, you will notice that some functions appear across different software. Pay attention to details since this can matter a lot come tax season.

Tip Number Fifteen: Always keep Printed Charts Handy.

Holding onto printed records is an invaluable trading tool, and a great way to learn as a trader. To do this you will:

- **Print and List:** Get the chart printed out, then write the reasons for your decision to enter the trade, along with the fundamental aspects that affected your choices. Go into as much detail as you possibly can, since you are going to refer back to these notes repeatedly, in the future. This is your chance to learn something from your past with trading.

- **Mark Entry and Exit:** You will list your points of entry and exit on the chart, filling in any comments that you feel are relevant to those decisions. Again, get as detailed as you can.

- **File the Record:** Keep this chart so you can go back to it in the future. Make sure you stay aware of your emotional responses in the trades. Did you make decisions based on fear? Greed? Were you overly anxious? Perhaps you were in an over-confident mood that day. All of this is relevant information that can be put to use in the future. Report all of this down.

Once you can look at your trades in an objective way, you can start developing the self-control needed to go through with your plans, rather than relying on whims and impulses of the moment. Seeing your moods listed, along with the decisions that they led to, will help you notice signals in the future and watch out for possible dangers. It will also help you decide when you are in the best frame of mind to engage in trading activity.

Tip Number Sixteen: Start Small and Gradually Increase.

When you're getting familiar with Forex trading, the key is to start out with smaller sums of money, gradually growing your account with the gains that you earn, rather than the money you deposit. This is one of the most valuable tips for forex trading. Begin small, using a low amount of leverage, and then add watch your account organically grow as you win on trades and profit. Many beginner traders make the mistake of thinking that they need to go big in order to win, or that you have to invest a lot to make a lot. While this might apply in the future, as a beginner trader, this is a disastrous attitude to have.

You don't need to have a larger account in order to get large returns. If you make a decision to grow the capital in your account by the choices you make in trades, that's great. If you don't do this, it's quite pointless to continue adding money to your account when it's burning through the capital. Instead, be smart about your money and develop an attitude of patience. Then, you can watch it grow exponentially.

<u>Tip Number Seventeen: Have a Narrow Focus at First.</u>

When you start out, keep your attention on just one pair of currency, only expanding as your skills improve. When it comes to trading currency, you should remember that this can be complex and deep, because of the chaos inherent in the trading market, along with the purposes and characters of the people participating in it. This makes it difficult to accurately predict or follow the various types of financial information being passed around.

It's a great idea, then, to hold our focus and activity of trading on just one currency pair at a time. This should be a pair we are familiar with and understand. Starting out with the currency of your own country can work great. But if this isn't what you wish to do, try to find the pair that is most widely traded and liquid. This will provide great practice for you.

Tip Number Eighteen: Only Trade what you Have an Understanding of.

This sounds simple, but failing to do this can be your undoing, as a trader. Essentially, if you aren't certain about what you're trading with, and can't defend your position and give good reasons for it to trusted critics, you should not make that trade.

- **Forget about Rumors:** Never trade because of some hot tip you heard or based on rumors and hearsay.

- **Be Aware of Consequences:** You should never act on a trade unless you are confident that you're aware of the positive possibilities, along with the possible negative consequences to your actions.

Tip Number Nineteen: Select your Methodology and stay Consistent in Applying it.

Before going through with entering the market, you should have ideas for the way you will make choices for your trading. You have to be aware of the information you'll need for knowing when to exit or enter different trades, ahead of time. Some traders decide to take a look at an economy or company's fundamental aspects, then consult charts to decide which is the most appropriate time to go through with trading.

Other traders may rely on technical methods for analysis, only relying on charts for timing their trades. Keep in mind that underlying fundamental aspects control trends over long periods of time, while patterns on charts could present opportunities for trading in shorter periods of time. No matter which method you decide to go with, stay consistent with it. Make sure that you choose an adaptive methodology that you can adjust as you progress on the road of trading and learn along the way. You also need a system that can hold up to the dynamics of the market which are constantly changing.

Tip Number Twenty: Keep Records of your Successes and Failures.

As time goes on in your trading journey, having a record for the history of your trading habits will give you valuable perspective on your skills, along with what needs work. This will give you a summary of every trade you've made, along with how your account looks in relation to separate trades, along with the effects of each trade you have made in the past.

It's your own personal data base for keeping tabs on your performance. This allows you to travel backwards in time to see when you traded, how it went, what pairs worked out for you and which did not, along with the time frames that offered the highest percentages of profit. You can be as analytical as you wish, which will allow you to gain a lot of valuable information from your records.

More Important Information to Have: The Bears and Bulls.

Even if you are quite new to the foreign exchange market, you have probably hear about the bears and bulls. Considering the situations of economics in both international situations and domestic situations, conditions constantly change, ebbing and flowing. This makes it possible to earn cash, regardless of the specifics of the market. In order to do that, you need to be aware of these important terms.

- **The Differences between the Two, put Simply:** All traders who wish to succeed should be aware of the differences between bears and bulls in foreign exchange. To put it simply, when the market is moving downward, it is considered to have bearish conditions, or be a bear market. When the market is moving upward, it's referred to as bullish, or a bull market. When a currency is going up in value, it's referred to as bullish. When it is going down in value, the currency is bearish.

- **A Reflection of the State of the Economy:** Bears and bulls in the foreign exchange market show the state of a country's economy.

- **The Economy of a Nation under Bullish Conditions:** Under bullish conditions, that economy is functioning well, including low rates of unemployment and affordable interest rates for citizens. Too much enthusiasm from investors has a tendency to lead to bull conditions that are exaggerated, leading the bubble of the market to burst open.

- **The Economy of a Nation under Bearish Conditions:** These happen when the economy is low, businesses start letting workers go, and people who invest begin to lose their trading confidence. At times, when things are very bad, a bear market that is exaggerated can cause panic in investors and lead to a crash, from people selling off stocks in a state of panic.

- **Earning Money in both Markets:** A lot of traders think that they can only earn profit when the market is bullish in forex. However, they can find chances when the market is showing bearish tendencies, as well. The trader just has to have an understanding of how each market works, in order to earn money this way.

- **Earning in Bull Times:** During times of a bullish market in forex, when the economy is flourishing and functioning great, investors tend to have extra cash to invest, leading them to purchase plenty. This will feed the situation of supplies being short, causing the prices to rise even more.

- **Earning in Bear Times:** When the market is in a bearish state, prices are going down and traders are investing their money in instruments that have fixed returns, like bonds. Since cash is being taken out of the market, supply will go beyond demand, causing prices to go down even more. At times, considering fluctuations in the long term, when the market is bearish, prices may go up as well, but not for long.

This means that when the market is in a bullish state, these are the best profit-earning conditions for investors and traders. If you manage to enter when it is just starting, you will have the potential to earn great profits. Keep in mind that downward trends in the wake of a bullish market will get corrected soon and are only temporary. Since prices are not able to go up infinitely, it's the investor's choice to decide when the market has reached its peak and when to sell accordingly.

Bearish markets give the perfect conditions to purchase at quality, affordable prices. This means that when you get in near the ending of a bearish market, you will enjoy the best chance for success in profit-earnings. Since prices usually go down before going back up, you should stay prepared for losing a bit in the short term. Selling short is a strategy used by investors when the market is bearish, and entails selling when you don't think the market will drop even more.

Stick to your Strategies for Risk Management:

As stated earlier, investors should be experienced, skilled, and have pre-decided strategies and techniques for protecting themselves against risk, no matter what the state of the market is. Strategies are only valuable when they are actually used, so develop the self-discipline needed to follow through on your methods.

Chapter 4: Forex Information you Need to Have

Tip Number Twenty One: Never Add More to a Position in the Red.

You should never, as a trader, add more money to a position that is losing. Although this may seem obvious, ignoring this very principle has led countless traders to financial ruin over history. No one can predict which way a currency pair will head within days or weeks worth of time. Although it's possible to make an educated guess, having no awareness of which way the price will head within the short term.

This means that you can only have certainty about the value of a trade right now, in the present. There is not much that you can say about future price movements. Therefore, it is never worth it to add money to a position that is losing, unless you're in this to gamble, that is. Although red positions can survive by themselves if they follow your pre-planned idea, adding more money to it is never recommended.

Tip Number Twenty Two: Record Trade Details before Executing the Plan.

Not only should you be recording the results of your trade history, but you should write detailed accounts of the plans you have for a trade, before you even enter it. This will let you think rationally about each decision before making it, and decide on specifications as to when and how you will enter, what risks you're willing to deal with, how much you wish to earn on the trade, and what you will do as the trade progresses.

Recording all of this is a great way to record ideas in real data, and strict numbers, making it easier to turn goals into actionable steps that can become profits. This will form the perfect basis for planning out the details of trading, and then putting it to use.

Tip Number Twenty Three: Get your Emotions in Check.

This is the downfall of many investors, and it's what separates the winners from the people who give up easily or end up losing due to rash decisions. Restraining your emotions is one of the most important aspects to being successful on the foreign exchange market.

- **It isn't just Negative Emotions to Watch for:** Panic, greed, and fear can take over your mind and lead you to make rash decisions, but it isn't just negative emotions that can get in the way. Excitement and euphoria can also cloud your judgment, and none of these feelings should be affecting the way you make your calculations and decisions.

- **Traders are Human:** Although this is pretty well-known at this point, traders are human, after all, so it isn't as easy as it sounds. We have to figure out methods for dealing with these feelings in the moment, while also letting them have a minimal impact on our lives and keeping them under control.

This is another reason why beginner investors should also start with smaller amounts of money. When your risk is low, it's easier to be calm, and keep your goals in mind, getting rid of the risk of emotions taking over your choices for trading. An approach that emphasizes logic and downplays intensity of emotions, is the way to win your way to a great forex trading career.

Tip Number Twenty Four: Be Aware of What Affects the Forex Market.

As a forex trader, you have to know about which factors influence the price changes of currency the most. Here are some of the main factors to keep an eye on and get educated about:

- **GDP:** Also known as the gross domestic product, the GDP refers to the dynamics and volume of what the government of a country or state is spending.

- **Budget Surpluses or Deficits:** This refers to aggregate investment on a private level, aggregate consumption, the amount of savings on a private level, and import and export volume.

- **Unemployment:** Unemployment percentages definitely influence currency pair price changes, along with inflation.

This may sound tedious, and not all traders want to spend their days studying this information. If this applies to you, you can follow along with what professional analysts of this information have to say. You can find that information online, on television, and radio. Many brokers also provide analytic information online, making the trading process simpler for investors.

- **The Mood of the Market:** Another important factor in analyzing the market is taking expectations of the public into account. This focuses on the emotions and mood of traders who are also participating in the forex market. As opposed to other types of analysis related to this, be learning how to read the expectations of the market, you are figuring out what traders expect and hope for in the future.

While trading, each investor has beliefs, which can affect the market in large groups. These moods comprise the whole expectation of the forex market, and being aware of these sentiments will help you understand the market movements better. Plenty of opinion pieces on this information exist online.

Tip Number Twenty Five: Stay Away from Magic Items.

Don't make the mistake of relying on gimmicks related to trading, such as wonder methods or forex robots. Unfortunately, products like this which have been untested and unproven are very popular. They make big bucks for the people selling the products, but hardly pay off at all for the buyers. It's easy to refute the reliability of these products. If the people who create these products have found such a magic answer, allow them to become rich off of them. If that doesn't happen, there's probably a reason.

Tip Number Twenty Six: Never work Against the Market.

You should not ever be working against the market. The exception to this is if you have the capital and patience to stand by your plan in the long term. Essentially, beginner traders should not ever go against trends, or try to pick bottoms and tops by working against the momentum present in the market at the time. Instead, go along with the current trends so you can let your mind get accustomed to this world and relax. If you try to go against trends, the fear and stress you experience will only set you back in the long run.

Tip Number Twenty Seven: Try to Automate Trading Behavior.

We have already gone over how important it is to control your feelings to make sure you have a profitable and successful career in forex trading. A great tip for minimizing rash decisions is to try automating your choices and behavior in trading, as much as you possibly can. No, this doesn't mean that you should try to use a robot for forex, or purchase expensive strategies for the technical stuff. What you should do is try to make your responses and choices similar in similar scenarios and situations. To put it another way, don't try to improvise, and instead allow your responses to events in the market follow along with a tested and studied plan of action.

Tip Number Twenty Eight: Open a Practice Account First.

Having knowledge doesn't get you anywhere if you can't practice with it. Whether you are curious or impatient to get into the market, you have to understand that to get an understanding of forex, you need a practice account first. Plenty of online resources exist that allow demo accounts free of deadlines. This will let you study what you need to know to be successful with real money in trading. Once you notice that most of your demo trades are successful, you are ready to enter the market and put real cash on the line. You should have placed a minimum of 20 fake trades on a platform before progressing to real money, so that you have plenty of time to become familiar with how the platform works.

Tip Number Twenty Nine: Become a Money Management Expert.

When you start to earn profits from trading in the foreign exchange market, you need to know how to keep them protected. Remember that the world of trading forex is a volatile and unpredictable one. You can lose money just as quickly as you earned it, so make sure you're being realistic and know how to manage these risks. Some traders make the mistake of getting too confident when they go on a winning streak, which can lead to carelessness and, eventually, losing money. Don't let this happen to you. Start good habits from the beginning.

Knowing how to manage your money entails minimizing your losses, maximizing your profits, and keeping your capital safe from harm. Every trader, in order to refrain from taking unnecessary gambles, has to know how to cut their losses and allow their profits to ride. We will talk more in detail about what it means to cut your losses, later on in this book.

Tip Number Thirty: Get Acquainted with Fundamental Analysis Techniques.

Another type of data collection and analysis that traders use is called fundamental analysis. This focuses on events and political news that will impact currency rates. One major difference with technical and fundamental analysis is that the fundamental method believes that currency prices directly reflect the supply and demand present at the time, which relies on fundamental economy aspects. Technical analysis, on the other hand, does not take into account reasons for changes in price, and instead focus on the history and dynamics of movements in prices. These types of factors come in two main groups:

- **Expected Events:** Economic indicators being published, to show important events that are coming up in the near future.

- **Unexpected Events:** These can never be forecasted, since revolutions in politics, terrorism, and natural disasters belong in this category.

Fundamental analysis states that trying to predict price changes is only possible when taking into account factors that directly influence demand and supply. Fundamental analysis pays a lot of attention to specific factors that will play a role in these changes.

More Important Information: How Confusing in Forex to Learn?

Different traders view the market of foreign exchange in various ways. While some believe that the forex market is complex and confusing, others believe that it's simple and no knowledge is needed. So which is the correct view?

They are, actually, both incorrect. The market is not difficult and complex, but people who are interested in trading must know about the market in order ot profit instead of lose. This doesn't mean that those educated in finance can succeed with Forex. Anyone who starts has to know the basics, first. You have to know how to analyze situations in the market, and then craft actions to take that fit the current situation. Apart from the analytical aspects involved here, beginners need to know that when they start out, they are always developing skills, and that there is no limit with how far you can advance.

There is always something new to be learned, even when you've been doing this for decades. The whole process of trading is risky, and people tend to lose at first because they jump into fast. Don't make this mistake. Become ready through gaining as much knowledge as you can and constantly learning.

Chapter 5: Do This, if you Want to be Successful

Although there is no "one size fits all" strategy for trading forex, there are many general guidelines that you should follow if you hope to be successful. With constant practice, you will be well on your way to a great trading career where all of your financial dreams become possible.

Tip Number Thirty One: Make sure your Expectations are Realistic.

It's true that the market of forex can make sudden shifts that were larger than you expected, but staying realistic is important. This means that you shouldn't expect to invest a couple hundred and end up earning a grand each time. Investing in the short term with smaller time frames will give you fewer opportunities for profit than long term investments, but it also comes with a considerably higher level of risk. With trading, there is always a matter of risk vs. reward.

Tip Number Thirty Two: Learn to Love Simplicity.

Learning how to keep things simple will benefit you exceedingly in the world of trading. Your analysis and trade plans should be both fully explained and understood by you. Trading foreign exchange is not as complicated as some believe. You don't have to be a genius at math or a financial expert to earn money using this method. Rather, having a clear vision and goals that have been defined in detail, will allow you to make your way toward success. The best way to achieve this is to resist overanalyzing, and never rationalize the areas that you made mistakes in.

Tip Number Thirty Three: Make sure your Trading Plan Includes...

You must have your plan set up before you even begin investing in real trades. You shouldn't ever follow another person's experience, because that was their own personal strategy that may not work out for your situation. Stay true to your own personal level of risk tolerance, views of the market, and stick with your personal plan. Every great plan includes the following:

- **Your Trading Objective:** This should be a specific, outlined target, along with the results you hope for and expect (as far as profit goes).

- **Strategies that are Proven:** For a strategy to be proven, it should be something that has worked for *you* personally, in your own experience. These should also include data that you use to make your decisions for when to enter and exit the forex market.

- **A System for Managing Risk:** To have a complete plan for trading, you have to form your own system for managing risk. This includes knowing ahead of time the level of risk that comes along with your trading position, as well as how much of your deposit you can afford to lose.

Tip Number Thirty Four: Never Give Up, and Keep your Plan Safe.

If you only risk what you can lose, stay determined to succeed, and act persistent, you will be in an advantaged position for trading. You probably won't become an expert at trading in just one day or week, so you must wait until your skills mature over the course of some weeks. Following these guidelines should have you succeeding within 30 days. Allow your talents to develop before you throw in the towel and decide that the trading life is not for you. Only invest amounts that won't completely ruin your future plans, and learning won't be dangerous or negative.

Tip Number Thirty Five: Work on Developing Confidence.

We've already briefly discussed how risky trading is. Regardless of the various methods that traders use to analyze the market, it's still a fact that no one can predict it right all the time. People invest their capital in this market and suffer disappointments due to the market turning in an unexpected way, which leads to losses. But the highest priority here is to stay mentally strong and balanced, because getting too down and insecure only heightens your risk of making mistakes. To be an effective trader, you have to stay as calm as you can. Some find picking up calming exercises to be helpful, such as meditation.

Tip Number Thirty Six: Always Use a Stop Loss.

A stop loss refers to an order than closes your position automatically when it hits a certain price. This serves to limit possible losses when you aren't able to watch the market. These are absolutely essential for managing your risk and also require practice to get them right. Some more information about stop losses:

- **Percentages:** You shouldn't ever risk over 20% of your entire account capital. Managing risk will help you stay away from extreme losses.

- **Pre-determine Risk:** Decide upon the size of your position based upon the amount you will be losing out on if your stop loss functions at the price you decided on. The amount should never go beyond the level of risk you already decided ahead of time.

Failing to follow through with stop losses is making a huge mistake, but newbies do it all the time. Having a tight stop loss means that your losses get cut before they can grow. This is an essential for beginning traders.

Tip Number Thirty Seven: Remember, it's your Money.

As a trader, you will encounter plenty of people (both online and in the real world) who want to give you advice and tell you their secrets. All of this should be taken with a grain of salt. Remember, trading is a personal journey, and no strategy suits all. Sure, it could be a good idea to talk about your beliefs related to the market with friends, but your decisions are yours, and yours alone, to make. Follow only your own, personal judgment. You can listen to others, but always make sure you're making a choice because it's right for you, not because someone told you to.

Tip Number Thirty Eight: Make sure Account info is Listed on the Platform.

When it comes time to decide which platform you should go with, you will find no shortage of options on the internet. Every company involved in finance will suggest at least one platform for trading. In addition to this, a company of finances that offers its very own trading platform probably has advantages over other choices. Every company in finance has multiple account type options. These are different due to the minimum amounts required for deposits, leverage ratios, and other considerations. And here's the important part: The exact details of how to open an account on a platform should be listed online, in plain English. If you don't make sure of this, you could run into problems later on.

Tip Number Thirty Nine: Never get Frozen into Inaction.

A common rookie mistake when people just start out trading in the foreign exchange market is allowing their losses at add up. Expert, successful traders know how to accept small losses fast if their trade isn't going as planned, in order to move on and benefit from a new opportunity. Traders who are unsuccessful, however, get frozen if their trade starts heading downward. Instead of taking fast actions to stop their losses, they might end up grasping the position, hoping that it will turn around and start going back up. This can be disastrous and lead to even higher, unnecessary losses.

On top of having money tied up, instead of being put to good use, getting frozen into inaction might result in severe losses to your trading account. Developing an easy going attitude that allows you to move on quickly, accepting your losses in stride, will go a long way.

Tip Number Forty: Develop Strong Self-Discipline.

Successful trading has a lot to do with self-discipline. This is knowing how to stay patient, and knowing when to wait until you have a proper point of entry. At times, you won't see that action in a price has reached the price point you decided on ahead of time. When this happens, you will need to have a discipline approach, to stay determined and strong with your planning system, and not go against it. This type of self-discipline also means knowing when and how to take action when you see indications that you should.

Considering all of the tips and tricks outlined in this chapter, you may be feeling enthusiastic about getting acquainted with such a compelling market. For many new traders, this could be an exciting and novel interest, meaning that you'll have to stay positive and patient in order to succeed. Use your time wisely and you will certainly learn how to profit from the foreign exchange market.

Chapter 6: Forex Guidelines to Take to Heart

Tip Number Forty One: Don't Trade too Often.

This tip may sound a bit counter-intuitive. After all, isn't more practice always better when you're new at something? Not always. Trading too often (also known as overtrading) can eat into your returns and turn great profits into devastating losses. Many expert traders have learned this the hard way, but trading too often can eat into returns in the long run. Remember, sometimes less is more and this is your chance to develop good habits early on.

Tip Number Forty Two: Never Overcompensate.

Attempting to average up (or down) in order to save a position that is losing can be a huge mistake. This might work for investors with long-term goals in mind, but for traders working with riskier, more volatile securities, this is simply ill-advised. Many of the largest losses of trading history have come about because the investor continued to add to a position that was losing, eventually needing to cut the whole position when losses grew to insufferable amounts. It's also possible to average up, due to an advancing security, rather than declining. This is just as risky, but equally common for new traders. Don't wait until you're deep into trading to make avoiding overcompensation a solid habit.

Tip Number Forty Three: Don't get Overconfident.

We already covered the importance of having a self-assured, confident demeanor while trading, but getting too confident can be just as damaging as having no confidence. Trading in the foreign exchange market can be highly demanding, and due to the luck that some beginners may experience, they are in danger of believing that this is a get rich quick scheme. This kind of attitude is risky since it encourages complacency and breeds risky behaviors that can lead to financial ruin or, at the very least, bad habits that will be hard to break later on.

Tip Number Forty Four: Always Stay Objective in your Trades.

Being able to maintain an emotionally detached state of mind is crucial for trading successfully in the forex market. This also depends entirely on how reliable your trading plans and systems are. If your system allows you levels of exit and entry that you can trust in the reliability of, you won't have to become easily influenced or overly emotional. Your plan needs to be so reliable that you can always have confidence following through with the signals you notice in regards to it.

Tip Number Forty Five: Treat your Demo Money like it's Real.

As soon as you have gotten the mechanics of forex trading down, you should open up a demo account on a platform so that you can find out what your style and personality for trading is. These platforms give you various choices between different styles and sizes to let you know. Maybe you're a short-term investor who prefers using higher leverage. Maybe you will end up liking smaller sizes better that could hold positions in the long term and eventually add up in points. Trading in a demo account, as we mentioned earlier in the book, will allow you to discover what style suits your personality.

But one thing you need to keep in mind is that you should treat the money in your demo account as though it's real. You may be tempted to see this as just a game or just practice, but it's actually important for developing habits that will stay with you during your entire trading career. It's also a valuable opportunity to learn about yourself. Seeing the money in your account as fake will lead you to making rash, over-the-top trading choices that you would never be okay with in real life. Sure, it might be fun to win a million dollars in the demo account, but this doesn't go a long way in teaching you how to be patient and successful with trading real capital.

Tip Number Forty Six: Realize that Trading Foreign Exchange relies on Probabilities.

Trading foreign exchange is all about probability and analyzing risk. There isn't one style or method that will always be profitable. To be successful, you must position yourself in a way that allows you to take losses in a harmless way, while multiplying profits and opportunities. This type of position can only occur when you know how to manage your allocations of risk, while paying respect to risk management and the probabilities of the market, and forgetting to take probabilities into consideration means that you are treating trading like gambling.

Tip Number Forty Seven: Don't go for too Much Leverage.

While leverage is important, there is definitely such a thing as too much. Leverage is great since it can heighten returns for quality trades, but it's also dangerous since it can heighten losses on trades that are losing. Traders who are just starting out might get excited about their leverage, particularly in the foreign exchange market. However, they might soon find out that having too much leverage can bring your capital to ruin on the turn of a dime.

Tip Number Forty Eight: Always Remember to Exercise Risk Control.

We've mentioned risk a few times already in this guide, because it's highly important. In fact, when it comes down to it, trading with success is more about controlling risk than anything else, and that is not an overstatement. Accept your losses without regret, if you have to experience them. Attempt to steer your trading the right way from the start. If it ends up backing off, cut off there and try another opportunity. Many times, it's after multiple attempts that you find your trade suddenly going the right way. Keeping this in mind takes a whole lot of discipline and patience, but when it happens, you can usually steer your trades in a profitable direction, or at least end up breaking even when you come out of the trade.

Tip Number Forty Nine: Stick to One Market at a Time.

Never make the newbie mistake of trading different markets at once. As a beginner, you might want to go between markets, testing them out, to figure out what you like best or what works for you. But doing this can just distract you and keep you from gaining valuable experience. The best thing you can do at this point is focus your attention on one area and excel in a specific type of market.

Tip Number Fifty: Always do your Trading Homework.

This may not be the most fun aspect of trading, but it's important. Don't put off doing your homework. Traders who are new often try to jump into trades without doing enough research. But you need to know about trends of the season, data release timing, and patterns in trading that all experts are aware of. Beginners often feel urgency toward starting a trade that can override the desire to research, but this can end up costing you a lot and wasting your time. There is no substitute for taking the time to acquire knowledge about a subject.

More Important Information to Have about Forex:

We have already covered our 50 tips, but here are some more important points to keep in mind for your trading journey.

- **Demos aren't just for Beginners:** After you've made the transition to live trading, you might be tempted to throw out your demo account, but trading on a demo account can still benefit you. This can be a way to test out new set ups and strategies to see if they work before risking them with real capital. Most traders know that if you can't win on a demo account, you probably won't win on the real account either.

- **Don't Follow the Herd:** Avoid the mistake of following trends or what everyone else is doing. This is a mistake that brings a lot of new traders down, so avoid it before you have to learn the hard (and expensive) way.

Trading can earn you a lot of money, as long as you follow the tips given to you in this book. It's true that all traders make mistakes every so often, but beginners should be especially careful, since they might not be able to bounce back as easily as more experienced traders. This is your chance to form good habits that will stick with you for the entirety of your career in trading foreign exchange. Good luck!

Conclusion

Thank you again for purchasing this book!

I hope this book was able to help you to see the possibilities of making money in the Forex trading market. Anyone with the right knowledge and attitude can make this a reality.

The next step is to use the tips and tricks given to you in this book and start building your pathway to success today! Remember that the best way to enjoy success is by growing your account organically, using profits, rather than adding more and more money out of your pocket. Keeping records of all of your trades, complete with printed out charts and notes about your entry and exit points, will help you become the best.

Finally, if you enjoyed this book, then I'd like to ask you for a favor, would you be kind enough to leave a review for this book on Amazon? It'd be greatly appreciated!

Click here to leave a review for this book on Amazon!

Thank you and good luck!

www.ingramcontent.com/pod-product-compliance
Lightning Source LLC
Chambersburg PA
CBHW070404190526
45169CB00003B/1100